Lion
Easter
Favourites

Stories and Prayers
for the season

LION
CHILDREN'S

Contents

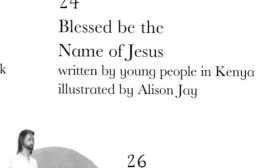

The Tale of Three Trees

retold by Mary Joslin

illustrated by Claire St Louis Little

Long ago, on a high hillside, stood three trees. With every passing year, they grew taller and stronger. In the spring, their roots drank in the cool raindrops that trickled through the soil. In the summer, they unfolded their leaves to the sun. In the autumn, strong winds swirled around their branches. In winter, they rested. Snow settled around their roots and on their branches. Under the cold night sky that glittered with a million stars, they dreamed their dreams.

The first tree spoke. 'My dream is of great riches,' it said. 'I want to make them mine and to hold them tight. I do not want to stay out here where the wind strips my branches bare each year; I want to be made into a beautiful chest that will hold the finest treasure.'

The second tree spoke. 'My dream is of great power,' it said. 'I want to have my way wherever I go. I do not want to stay out here rooted to the soil. I want to be made into a mighty sailing ship, and for the world's mightiest kings to put their life into my hands when they sail the great oceans.'

The third tree sighed, and shivered as a chill breeze shook its branches. 'I want to stay here for ever,' it said. 'I want to point to the vast and beautiful heavens, and to the mysteries that lie beyond them.'

Many years went by, and the trees grew ever taller. Then, one winter's day, three woodcutters climbed the hill, and each one had an axe.

'This tree has wood that will last for years,' said the woodcutter who stood under the first tree. He lifted his axe.

'Now I shall hold great treasure,' thought the first tree, and it fell to the ground.

'This tree has wood that is hard and strong,' said the woodcutter who stood under the second tree. He lifted his axe.

'Now I shall carry kings across the sea,' thought the second tree, and it fell to the ground.

'This tree has grown very tall,' said the woodcutter who stood under the third tree. He lifted his axe. 'Now my dream is already over,' wept the third tree, and it fell to the ground.

A carpenter took the wood from the first tree, sawed it into planks, then joined them – not into a chest, but into a trough for cattle-feed. The farmer filled it with hay for his slow, dreamy-eyed oxen. 'What has happened to my dream?' wondered the tree.

One night, the animals were led aside and a man and a woman took shelter in the stable. Soon, gentle hands put fresh, clean straw in the trough, and a new-born baby was laid upon it. Then the first tree knew that it was holding the greatest treasure the world had ever known.

A shipwright took the wood from the second tree. He sawed it and shaped it into a small boat. Fishermen cast their nets from it into a violet blue lake and dragged in their catch of slithering fish. 'What has happened to my dream?' wondered the tree.

One night, storm winds blew and great waves crashed. Then a man stood up in the boat and spoke to the storm: 'Peace. Be still.' At once there was calm, and the second tree knew that it was carrying the mightiest king the world had ever known.

The wood from the third tree was roughly hewn and left in a woodyard. But the tree had already given up dreaming.

Years passed. The wood was almost forgotten. Then, one day, came a clamour of voices: 'Any wood will do, but fetch it quickly!'

Rough hands grasped the wood of the third tree, and made it into a cross. Cruel hands forced a man onto the timbers. Soldiers fastened him to the wood, with nails through his hands and his feet. Then they hoisted the cross upright. There, on a low, barren hilltop, the man died.

Three days later, a bright day dawned.

As a gentle morning breeze blew, the tree knew that everything had changed: the man who had died was alive again. Death was no more.

From that day on, whenever people looked at the cross, they lifted their eyes to the vast and beautiful heavens and thought of the mysteries that lie beyond them.

God's Springtime Garden

Three poems by Lois Rock
illustrated by Alex Ayliffe

God is waking the world again
Cold and frost are going.

God is waking the world again
New green leaves are growing.

God is waking the world again
Warmer winds are blowing.

God is waking the world again
Springtime flowers are showing.

Baby creatures, just awakened,
You are part of God's creation;
Baby creatures, oh, so small,
God is father of us all.

In the Easter garden
the leaves are turning green;
in the Easter garden
the risen Lord is seen.

In the Easter garden
we know that God above
brings us all to heaven
through Jesus and his love.

The Tale of the Heaven Tree

by Mary Joslin
illustrated by Meilo So

In the beginning, the world's Great Maker planted a garden.
Its different fields were each filled with many lovely plants.

There were woodland gardens, deep in green moss and shyly nodding bellflowers, where little creatures snuffled and rustled.

There were prairie gardens, rippling with grasses, where animals ran and leaped with graceful strides.

There were undersea gardens for the creatures of the deep, with trailing leaves drifting in the water currents and mysterious flowers with swaying petals.

Most lovely of all were the gardens of tall trees that reached to the sky and were a home for all the birds to live in. Their leafy branches were filled with chirruping and twittering, warbling and whistling, tumbling, trilling melodies to delight the world.

The Great Maker asked people to take care of the world, and to build for themselves simple, safe dwellings in any of the gardens that pleased them.

But time passed, and the people grew greedy…

'Let us build for ourselves bigger homes!' they said.

'There are building materials in abundance, and they are for us to use as we like.'

Soon they were building palaces.
Each new building towered above the last, and the palaces were made ever more magnificent.

Their thousands of rooms were filled with every kind of luxury… but the people's greed could never be satisfied.

The gardens of the world were ruined, each a scene of the most pitiful devastation.

All the trees had been cut down.

The birds fluttered wretchedly on the cold ground, desperately trying to make new homes.

Their songs were silenced.

Then a small child looked from the top of her palace home down on the devastated world, and she wept.

'Go down to the earth,' whispered the voice of the Maker in the wind. 'There you will find a seed, and you must plant it where it can grow safely.'

So the child ran down the winding staircase of the tower, down and down and down.

There, on the earth, was a seed: brown, wrinkled, ugly.

The child took the seed gently in her hand. 'Where will it be safe?' she wondered.

As she walked along, she came to a ditch where dark mud oozed and a few reeds were bending in the chill wind.

'Here, where no one ever comes,' the wind seemed to whisper.

And there she buried the seed.

Slowly, silently, and all unseen, the seed began to grow.

It grew into a strong tree.

Beneath its branches, new gardens began to flourish.

Soon, the creatures gathered around it.

It grew taller than any palace, and the birds of the air flew among its branches and built their nests in it.

It grew so tall it reached to Heaven, and any who wished could climb its branches into the Great Maker's garden paradise.

In the Court of Pontius Pilate

retold from the Bible by Trevor Dennis
illustrated by Christina Balit

The morning had arrived. It was time to send Jesus to Pilate. So the priests tied Jesus' hands together and led him through the streets to the palace where Pilate was staying during the festival.

Pilate was delighted that they'd managed to arrest Jesus without causing any disturbance in the city. He knew why they'd been so keen to get their hands on the man, but he didn't worry about any of that. All he was interested in was the report he'd received from his own troops, that the Galilean was going round calling himself a king, and that he had a large crowd of followers who believed he was. Apparently, some children had been shouting, 'God bless the king!' inside the precincts of the temple. Clearly he had to get rid of the

man, or he'd have a major riot on his hands, and the emperor back in Rome wouldn't be pleased at all. The emperor didn't like riots.

Jesus was led into his presence. Pilate looked him up and down. His hands were tied, and his face was bruised and swollen with the beating he'd had from the temple guards. He could see people had been spitting on him.

'So,' he said, with a sneer in his voice, '*you* are this king I've been hearing about, are you?'

'So you say,' said Jesus.

The chief priests leaped in at once with their accusations. Pilate expected Jesus to defend himself. But he didn't. He seemed to know the game they were playing and was having nothing to do with it.

'Have you nothing to say?' Pilate asked angrily. 'Look at all the charges they're bringing against you!'

Jesus remained silent. Pilate was astonished. In his experience Jewish troublemakers usually had a great deal to say for themselves. But this man clearly wasn't frightened.

'Well, we'll have to see what the crowd thinks, won't we?' he said.

They were in an upstairs room, overlooking a large courtyard at the front of the palace. The courtyard was seething with people. Pilate looked down on them all. He had nothing but contempt for them. And yet he was still afraid of them. If some of them were supporters of this strange, silent Galilean, then they could turn very nasty when he condemned him to death. It was a tricky situation.

Fortunately, he had an idea. There was a man under guard in the palace, called Barabbas. He was a leader of the Dagger Men. The Dagger Men, in the eyes of the Romans, were notorious Jewish terrorists. Barabbas and his gang had caused a riot and had stabbed several Roman soldiers to death. Pilate was waiting to have them crucified after the festival, once the pilgrims had gone home. But perhaps he could let Barabbas off after all. Barabbas was a broken

man. The Roman torturers had done their work well. He wouldn't cause any more trouble, and the rest of his gang would be executed anyway. Pilate knew he wouldn't be taking any real risk if he released him. But the crowd wouldn't know that, of course. They'd like it if Barabbas was set free. He often released one of his prisoners at Passover, to keep the crowds happy. They'd come to expect it. This time he could give them a choice: Barabbas or Jesus. They could choose the one they liked best, only he and the priests would see to it they got Barabbas. Yes, Pilate thought to himself, this could work out very nicely. He gave orders for Barabbas to be fetched from the dungeons. Then he went over to the priests and explained his plan. The priests left the room and went outside to mingle with the crowd.

There was a large platform out in the courtyard, and in the middle of it a grand seat like a throne. Some soldiers escorted Pilate to the platform, and he sat down. More soldiers came behind him, leading Jesus and Barabbas.

'As you see,' Pilate called out, pointing to Jesus, 'I've got your precious king. Would you like me to set him free for you?'

'No, Barabbas!' the crowd shouted.

Those priests have done a good job, thought Pilate. 'Then what shall I do with this king?' he said to the crowd.

'Crucify him!' they yelled.

'Why,' said Pilate, pretending to be horrified, 'what's he done wrong?'

The crowd yelled all the louder, 'Crucify him! Crucify him!'

My word, said Pilate to himself. Those priests are clever! Crucifixion's a Roman punishment. Getting Jews to call for a Jew to be crucified!

Whoever heard of such a thing? The priests have got them completely hysterical.

'Very well,' he said to the crowd, 'I'll do as you say.' He turned to the soldiers. 'Let Barabbas go. As for this Jesus, give him a good flogging and then crucify him.'

He got down from the platform and went inside the palace to get on with his work. It had all gone remarkably smoothly, he thought.

Blessed be the Name of Jesus

written by young people in Kenya
illustrated by Alison Jay

Blessed be the name of Jesus,

who died to save us.

Blessed be Jesus,

who had compassion on us.

Blessed be Jesus,

who suffered loneliness, rejection and pain,

for our sakes.

Blessed be Jesus,

through whose cross I am forgiven.

Lord Jesus, deepen my understanding

of your suffering and death.

The
Easter Story

retold by Lois Rock from the Gospel of Matthew
illustrated by Diana Mayo

The little donkey picked its way down the stony track that led into the valley. It was nervous at being ridden for the first time and a little scared of the crowds all around.

Many people were making their way to Jerusalem, high on the hill ahead. The Passover festival was coming, and everyone wanted to be at the Temple in Jerusalem for the celebrations.

People began to notice who was riding the donkey.

'It's Jesus from Galilee,' a woman whispered.

'The preacher whom everyone is talking about.'

'You mean the one they say can work miracles,' said another.

'He can. I've seen it happen. He makes blind people see, and crippled people get up and walk.'

Jesus quietly continued his journey, his twelve disciples gathered around him.

The whispering began to spread. 'Healing people is something that the Messiah will be able to do,' someone said grandly, proud of what they knew.

Another added, 'Some people believe Jesus is our people's Messiah. That means he's going to be a king like our great King David of old.'

'That's right,' said a third, 'the king God has promised to send to save us from our enemies – the Romans who rule us and make us pay them taxes.'

He thought for a moment, then shouted aloud, 'Praise to David's Son! God bless him who comes in the name of the Lord!'

Then it seemed that everyone took up the cry. 'Praise God!' they cheered. Suddenly, Jesus was the centre of a great welcome. Some people threw their coats on the path for his donkey to walk on. Others cut branches from the palm trees by the side of the road to make the way smooth.

As Jesus rode through the valley and up the hill to the city gate, there was a joyful uproar.

Jesus went straight to the Temple. In the crowded courtyard that surrounded it, people were buying and selling. There were animals for sale – cattle and sheep and pigeons that could be offered as sacrifices during the festival. Added to the noise of the animals was the arguing and the haggling. Money jingled as people bought the special coins they needed to pay their Temple taxes, and the sellers smiled broadly as they pocketed huge profits.

Jesus watched, his face clouding over with anger. Then, quite deliberately, he went and pushed a stall over, scattering the coins. He turned and spoke aloud, his voice ringing out: 'It is written in the Scriptures that God said, "My Temple will be called a house of prayer." But you are making it a hideout for thieves!'

Then he tipped up another stall and upset a stool. The disturbance frightened the animals, who began to run.

'Get out!' Jesus shouted to the stallholders. 'All of you, get out.' He began to drive them away and refused to let the selling go on.

The chief priests came up to see what was happening.

'What do you think you're doing in our Temple?' they raged. 'And why are you letting people treat you as if you were the Messiah? It's got to stop.'

Jesus had no intention of stopping. For the next few days, he and his disciples came right into the city and spoke to the crowds: telling stories and answering all the questions that hecklers threw at him.

'We have a good question,' said some. They were Pharisees – people who had studied the Scriptures very carefully and tried to follow all the laws that God had given their people. They were sure that Jesus was not wise enough to answer questions about the Law.

'Teacher,' one of them asked Jesus, 'which is the greatest commandment in all of the Law that God has given us?'

Jesus spoke without hesitation: '"Love the Lord your God with all your heart, with all your soul, and with all your mind." This is the greatest and the most important commandment. The second most important commandment is like it: "Love your neighbour as you love yourself."'

Everyone recognized that Jesus was quoting the Scriptures to them. There was nothing in his reply that anyone could say was wrong. His wisdom only served to make them more angry.

The Pharisees and other teachers of the Law talked to the chief priests of their anger, and soon these powerful people were plotting to get rid of Jesus. Then came the chance they needed: one of Jesus' disciples came to visit them secretly. For thirty pieces of silver, Judas Iscariot arranged to let them know where they could come and find Jesus alone.

Jesus knew he was in for trouble, and he warned his disciples. Still, he wanted to share the special Passover meal with them.

He wanted to make this last supper together especially memorable. While they were eating, Jesus took a piece of bread, said a prayer of thanks, broke the bread and gave it to his friends. 'Take and eat,' he said; 'this is my body.'

Then he took a cup of wine, gave thanks to God, and gave it to them. 'Drink it, all of you,' he said; 'this is my blood… poured out for many for the forgiveness of sins.'

Although they did not fully understand, it was something they remembered for ever.

When the meal was over, they sang a hymn and went out of the city. 'You will all leave me tonight,' Jesus warned them sadly.

'I won't,' said the one called Peter boldly.

Jesus replied, 'Before tomorrow you will deny three times that you know me.'

In sombre mood, they made their way across the valley to a quiet olive grove called Gethsemane. There, Jesus went off on his own to pray.

He was fearful and unhappy, for he knew only too well what lay ahead.

'My Father, if it is possible, take this cup of suffering from me!' he asked God. Then he added, 'Yet not what I want, but what you want.'

Jesus continued praying while his disciples slept. Then, in the darkest night, Judas arrived. He had slipped away, and was returning with a band of armed men sent by the chief priests. 'Arrest the one to whom I give a kiss of greeting,' he whispered.

The rest of the disciples ran off, and Jesus was marched away. The chief priests and the teachers of the Law had gathered in the High Priest's house, ready with lies.

Peter followed at a distance. He sat outside while Jesus faced his accusers and, as time passed and there was no news, Peter felt his courage failing. Then a servant noticed him. 'You were with that Jesus,' she said, 'the one they have on trial inside the house.'

'I was not!' retorted Peter, suddenly very afraid indeed.

Shortly afterwards, another servant saw him and said the same.

'I don't know the man,' he swore.

Then one of the men came out. 'You must be one of Jesus' friends,' he said. 'Your accent shows that you're from Galilee just like him.'

Peter was terrified. 'I do not know the man!' he thundered.

Then the cock crowed as the dawn broke. Peter remembered Jesus' warning, and he went away weeping.

By now, the priests had made up their minds that they had all the reasons they needed in asking for Jesus to be put to death. Judas, suddenly sorry, could do nothing to stop them. Jesus was marched to the Roman governor, Pontius Pilate, the one who had to pass the official sentence of execution.

Pilate was puzzled by the demand. He was used to violent rebels – people who wanted to overthrow the Romans and make themselves King of the Jews. But Jesus wasn't like that. He seemed quiet and peaceable. So what was Pilate to do?

He decided to please the crowds who had gathered. It was the custom for him to release a prisoner at Passover time, and he could ask them to make their choice.

'It could be this Jesus,' he said, 'or Barabbas, whose many crimes are well known to you all.'

The chief priests had done their work well.

'Free Barabbas!' shouted the crowds.

'And Jesus?' asked Pilate.

'Crucify him! Crucify him!' they shouted in a frenzy.

Pilate's soldiers took Jesus. They dressed him in a scarlet robe and made a crown of thorny branches for his head.

'What a fine king you are now,' they mocked. They bowed down to him and sneered, 'Long live the King of the Jews.' Then they spat at him and hit him before giving him back his own clothes and marching him to the hill outside the city.

There, they crucified him, along with two bandits. Above his head they nailed the accusation against him: 'This is Jesus, the King of the Jews.'

People gathered to jeer: 'He trusts in God and claims to be God's Son. Let us see if God wants to save him now.'

Nothing happened except that the sun rose higher. Then, at noon, the sky went dark.

At three o'clock, Jesus cried out 'My God, my God, why did you abandon me?' Moments later, he died.

At once, the earth itself trembled and the curtain that screened the innermost and most holy part of the Temple was torn in two. People claimed that strange things were happening – that old tombs were opening and the dead walking. Surely this was no ordinary day.

The soldiers themselves were terrified. 'This man truly was the Son of God,' they whispered.

Several women who had come with Jesus from Galilee to help him in his work came a little closer, weeping as the sun sank low.

A rich man named Joseph from the town of Arimathea came and asked Pilate for the body of Jesus. He took it down and had it taken to a tomb cut in the rock. As two of the women watched, the stone door of the tomb was rolled into place.

The sun was setting, and the sabbath day of rest beginning.

After the sabbath, as Sunday morning was dawning, the two women who had watched Jesus being buried went to look at the tomb. They were Mary Magdalene and another Mary. Suddenly, there was an earthquake. An angel came down from heaven and rolled the stone away from the door of the tomb. The guards who had been ordered to keep watch were overcome with fear.

Then the angel spoke to the women: 'Do not be afraid. I know you are looking for Jesus, who was crucified. He is not here, he is risen.'

The women ran to tell the rest of Jesus' close friends, terrified and yet full of hope and joy. Suddenly, there before them was Jesus himself.

A great reunion took place in Galilee before Jesus went back to heaven. Jesus' faithful disciples met with him on a hill top. He told them to travel to every part of the world and spread the news.

'Teach people to be my followers, just as you are my followers,' Jesus said. 'Baptize them in the name of the Father, the Son and the Holy Spirit, and teach them to obey everything I have commanded you. And I will be with you always, to the end of the age.'

Miracle Morning

A story and two poems
illustrated by Francesca Pelizzoli

Jesus was dead. No one felt the pain of loss more keenly than the one they called Mary Magdalene. She remembered the old days before she met Jesus – her wild life, her wild temper, her wild hatred. Jesus had been a friend unlike any other. He had helped her to change, to become the person she had dreamt of being.

Now weeping, she returned to the tomb with a group of women while the sky was still dark.

As Mary drew nearer and could make out the shapes of the objects around it, her heart lurched. The stone was rolled back. The tomb was open. Someone had been there already. Fear and terror chilled her.

And then she ran – she needed help, and quickly. Simon Peter and John, Jesus' friends – they needed to know. They needed to do something. 'They have taken Jesus from the tomb!' she cried. 'We don't know where they have taken him.' The two men leaped up and raced to the tomb… John reached the mouth of the cave and stopped in amazement.

Peter rushed on… there were the cloths used to wrap the body; they were empty. Jesus had gone from the tomb. They looked around, wild-eyed. Was this a trap? Could this event have a simple, reasonable explanation? But there were no clues to be found, so they went away.

Mary stood behind, weeping. Tears dimmed her eyes. Why was the body not in the tomb? Perhaps if she looked again it would all be different.

Then she saw them… two figures dressed in shining white… angels. 'Woman, why are you crying?' they asked.

They have taken my Lord away,' she wept, 'and I do not know where they have put him.'

She turned around. A man was passing. He asked the same question: 'Why are you crying? Who are you looking for?'

Mary thought it must be the man who tended the little grove. Perhaps he had seen what happened.

'Oh, if you have taken Jesus' body, please tell me where it is and I will go and get him,' she begged.

'Mary,' said the man.

Then she knew. It was Jesus.

He was alive.

Retold from John 20:1–16

When Mary Thro' the Garden Went

When Mary thro' the garden went
There was no sound of any bird,
And yet, because the night was spent,
The little grasses lightly stirred,
The flowers awoke, the lilies heard.

When Mary thro' the garden went
The dew lay still on flower and grass,
The waving palms about her sent
Their fragrance out as she did pass,
No light upon the branches was.

When Mary thro' the garden went,
Her eyes, for weeping long, were dim,
The grass beneath her footsteps bent,
The solemn lilies, white and slim,
These also stood and wept for him.

When Mary thro' the garden went,
She sought, within the garden ground,
One for whom her heart was rent,
One for whom her sake was bound,
One who sought and she was found.

Mary Coleridge (1861–1907)

Rejoice at Easter

A poem and a prayer
illustrated by Ruth Rivers

The whole bright world rejoices now:
with laughing cheer! with boundless joy!
The birds do sing on every bough:
Alleluia!

Then shout beneath the racing skies:
with laughing cheer! with boundless joy!
To him who rose that we might rise:
Alleluia!

God, Father, Son and Holy Ghost:
with laughing cheer! with boundless joy!
Our God most high, our joy, our boast:
Alleluia!

Easter carol (17th century)

Merrily, merrily,
All the spring,
Merrily, merrily
Small birds sing.
All through April,
All through May,
Small birds merrily
Carol all day.

Rodney Bennett

35

Peter the Fisherman

by Joyce Denham

illustrated by Judy Stevens

Peter had a habit of jumping into the sea.

The first time was extremely risky, downright foolhardy, his friends thought. They were crammed into one of Peter's small fishing boats, all twelve of Jesus' disciples. It was dark and they were exhausted. All day, thousands of people had been following Jesus, begging him to heal their children, asking him to preach, hanging on his every word.

'You must rest,' Jesus had told the twelve. 'Jump into the boat and get away while I send the crowds home.'

They knew it would take hours to cross the huge lake, even longer now that the wind had turned against them. As the night wore on the men grew nervous: the air smelled of danger; the sea was stirring. At about three in the morning, the storm broke hard upon them. High into the air the seething waters heaved their boat; it teetered on the crest of the wave, then plunged into the deep trough.

'We're going to die!' they shouted in terror.

'What's that?' screamed Andrew, as a human figure appeared before them on the water.

'It's a spirit!' the men cried in horror. 'We're doomed!'

But the 'spirit' assured them: 'Don't fear!'

it said. 'I'm here! You're safe now!'

Is it true? thought Peter. Dare I believe that Jesus has come to us on the sea?

'Lord,' he called, 'if it's truly you, let me walk to you on the water!'

'Come!' Jesus replied, beckoning.

Instantly Peter was over the side of the boat, walking on the water! Running on the water! But the waves were so huge. He looked around in terror – and then he was sinking, gasping for breath. 'Lord, save me!' he cried.

Jesus grabbed him with strong arms and pulled him up. 'What happened to your faith?' he asked. 'What made you start doubting?'

They climbed into the boat. At once the sea was calm, and Peter looked at Jesus in amazement. 'Truly you are the Son of God!' he said. Never again would he doubt his Lord, he told himself. Never again would he give in to fear, no matter how terrifying the events.

After that, Peter's faith was firm: he had left everything to follow Jesus. The other disciples admired his boldness, his passion for God's truth, his reckless devotion to the Lord.

Then everything changed. That night when they were all together, eating the Passover supper, Jesus himself said those shocking words: 'One of you will betray me to the authorities tonight. I will be arrested, and all of you will desert me.'

Peter broke the stunned silence. 'No, Lord! Not me! I will never desert you!'

'Oh, Peter,' Jesus had answered him, 'if only I could spare you from what is to come. Satan, the evil one, will fight for your soul tonight. But I am praying for you. And

when you turn back to me, I want you to strengthen your fellow believers.'

'No, Lord,' Peter had protested. 'Even if the others give in to fear and forsake you, I never will.'

'Ah,' said Jesus, 'before the cock crows twice in the early dawn, you will have denied me three times.'

'I will never deny you!' Peter had vowed. 'I will die for you if I have to!'

So what was the new feeling of fear that swept over him as later that night he waited, sick with anxiety, outside the home of the high priest?

After the Passover supper, they had gone to a quiet garden where Jesus could be alone to pray. Never had Peter seen him so troubled. The next thing he knew there was a terrible commotion. (How could I have fallen asleep? he thought with dismay.)

There were Roman soldiers everywhere – and officers from the temple, even the chief priests and elders! Swords drawn! Torches blazing in the night! Swiftly the men seized Jesus and bound him.

Into the dark night the disciples fled. But as the guards led Jesus away, Peter followed. He slipped silently between buildings, moved in and out of the shadows, then ever so slyly found a place at the campfire in the courtyard of the high priest's residence – where they were questioning Jesus. He stood among the servants, trying to look like one of them; but a nagging fear, like a snake, slithered into his soul.

The fire leaped and danced. One of the servant girls was staring at him. 'You're one of his followers, aren't you?' she said.

His palms sweated; his heart pounded. 'No, I'm not!' he was saying. 'I don't know the man!'

'Yes you do!' the other servants joined in. 'Your accent gives you away – you sound like a Galilean!'

Waves of fear towered over him. 'I'm telling you, I've never met him!'

'You're one of them!' the guards shouted. 'One of his disciples!'

The sea of terror broke over him, choking him, sucking him under.

'No! I do not know him!' he growled.

The shrill scream of the cock broke the shadowy dawn, once, twice. Oh, Lord! he cried in his heart. How can you save me now? And he fled the scene, the burning tears streaming down his face.

The next day, Jesus was crucified, nailed to a cross of wood while his friends stood at a distance. After his body was buried, the disciples stayed in hiding. When some women went back to the tomb, they claimed that the body had gone and that Jesus had risen from the dead. Peter thought they had lost their senses. Then Jesus appeared to several of them. So it was true! But Peter felt more lost than ever, like being alone on a drifting ship, looking for others to help him to shore.

Later, Peter and the others were back in Galilee. They went out in Peter's boat, wondering what would happen next. All night they fished and caught nothing. They were so discouraged.

In the early dawn a man called to them

from the shore. 'Did you find fish?' he asked.

'No!' they shouted.

'Then put your net down on the other side of the boat!'

Something made them obey the stranger. Suddenly they caught so many fish they wondered if they could haul them to shore.

Then Peter realized who the man was: Jesus, the Lord. He leaped from the boat into the cold water, and swam to shore – where Jesus was waiting for them, cooking breakfast over a fire. Soon they all ate their fill, singing and laughing with delight.

After this, Peter's faith never wavered.

For the rest of his life he spoke boldly, encouraging those who believed in Jesus. He gave his life to spread the news Jesus brought – that love can conquer evil – and to pass on Jesus' promise of a new life, free from the fear of death.

A day came when Peter, too, was seized by Roman soldiers and put on trial for his faith. But Jesus had prayed for him. Even when his executioners came to do their worst, he stood firm. Billows of pain broke over his head. Seas of fear swept under him. 'Lord, save me!' he cried victoriously, and he didn't sink.

Easter is About

A prayer by Lois Rock

illustrated by Gail Newey

Good Friday is about

burdens loaded on innocent shoulders

and nails hammered into innocent hands,

a spear piercing an innocent heart

and death enshrouding an innocent life.

Easter is about

unexpected and joyful reunions

and simple meals shared with friends,

old grievances forgiven and forgotten

and angels rolling wide the way to heaven.

I Wish Tonight

by Lois Rock
illustrated by Anne Wilson

The evening sky darkens, the stars will shine bright,
But which is the first star that I'll see tonight?
I wish that I may, oh, I wish that I might
Have everything that I wish for tonight.

I wish for a silver moon sailing on high
Through the shape-shifting oceans of clouds in the sky
And a warm gentle breeze that will sing and will sigh
In the tall swaying treetops as it passes by.

I wish for a bed with a sail and an oar
That will float on the shadows so dark on the floor;
As the wind fills the sails to the sky it will soar
And take me up high to a faraway shore.

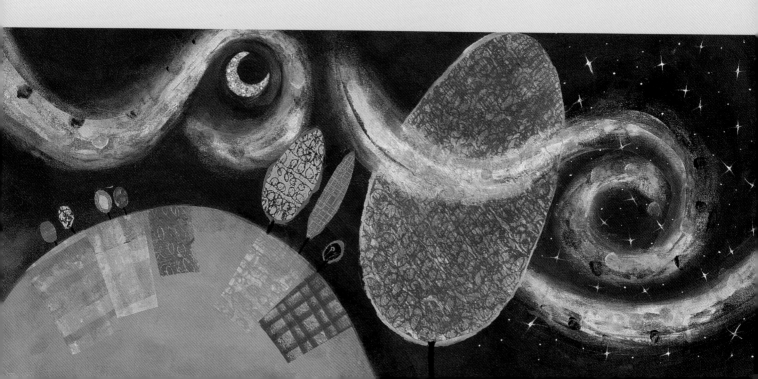

In the land of beyond all my dreams will come true.
I'll do all the things that I so want to do;
I'll have great adventures the whole long day through...
So I'll wish for my friends to be there with me too.

All the things that we need will be ours just for free
With enough for my friends – oh, and their friends – and me,
We'll pick what we want just like fruit from a tree;
Everyone in the world will come nearer to see.

We'll tell them that nothing can be bought or sold:
In the land that I wish for no one will need gold.
We'll pick lovely presents for young and for old
So no one goes hungry, and no one is cold.

43

Then one to another we'll say, 'Let's be friends,
And let's make a great plan: that together we'll mend
Anything that is broken, and carefully tend
Everything in the world; keep it safe to the end.'

Soon, no one will know where the wastelands have been:
The trees will grow tall and the deserts turn green,
The air will blow clear and the rain will fall clean,
And in shimmering streams silver fish will be seen.

The animals then will draw close without fear –
The shy little shrew will be first to come near,
Then musk ox, okapi, wapiti and deer.
Imagine the squeaking, the grunting, the cheer!

Then I'll call for quiet: 'Hush, everyone, please,
Let's listen to songbirds high up in the trees,
And after they've finished, the soft sighing breeze,
The rippling brooks, and the tumbling seas.'

I'll go down to the shore in the gold evening light
And climb back on my boat, sail off in the night,
While the skies turn to dark and the stars shine so bright
And I'll wish for a world where what's wrong is put right.

And then, in the morning, I'll wake with the sun,
My dream won't be over, my dream's just begun:
A dream full of goodness and laughter and fun
For me, for the world, and for everyone.

Compiled by Lois Rock
This edition copyright © 2006 Lion Hudson
Text and illustrations copyright: see acknowledgments below

The moral rights of the authors and illustrators
have been asserted

A Lion Children's Book
an imprint of
Lion Hudson plc
Mayfield House, 256 Banbury Road,
Oxford OX2 7DH, England
www.lionhudson.com
ISBN-13: 978-0-7459-4992-5
ISBN-10: 0-7459-4992-4

First edition 2006
10 9 8 7 6 5 4 3 2 1 0

A catalogue record for this book is available
from the British Library

Printed and bound in China

Acknowledgments

Cover (clockwise from top left): Gail Newey, Diana Mayo, Anne Wilson, Gail Newey, Alison Jay, Christina Balit, Judy Stevens, Anne Wilson, Ruth Rivers, Alex Ayliffe. Picture in centre by Diana Mayo. Copyright © individual illustrators listed above.
Endpages: 'The Springtime World' by Christina Goodings first published in *This Amazing World*. Text copyright © 2002 Lion Hudson. Illustrations for 'The Springtime World' and 'The Great Unseen' from *This Amazing World* copyright © 2002 Ruth Rivers.
The Tale of Three Trees: Text by Mary Joslin first published in *Celebrating Christmas*. Copyright © 1998 Lion Hudson. Illustrations copyright © 1998 Claire St Louis Little.
God's Springtime Garden: 'God is waking the world again' and 'In the Easter garden' by Lois Rock first published in *My Very First Prayers*. Copyright © 2003 Lion Hudson. Illustrations copyright © 2003 Alex Ayliffe. 'Baby Pets' by Lois Rock first published in *The Lion Book of 1000 Prayers for Children*. Copyright © 2003 Lion Hudson.
The Tale of the Heaven Tree: First published by Lion as a picture story book with this title in 1999. Text copyright © 1999 Lion Hudson. Illustrations copyright © 1999 Meilo So.
In the Court of Pontius Pilate: Text by Trevor Dennis first published in *The Book of Books*, copyright © 2003 Trevor Dennis. Illustrations from *The Lion Bible: Everlasting Stories* copyright © 2001 Christina Balit.

Blessed be the Name of Jesus: Poem by the young people of Kenya from *Pray With Us*, compiled by Maureen Edwards, published by Lion Hudson. Illustrations from *The Lion Treasury of Children's Prayers* copyright © 1999 Alison Jay.
The Easter Story: First published by Lion as a picture story book with this title in 2002. Text by Lois Rock, copyright © 2002 Lion Hudson. Illustrations copyright © 2002 Diana Mayo.
Miracle Morning: Story by Mary Joslin first published in *Miracle Maker*. Copyright © 1998 Lion Hudson. Illustrations copyright © 1998 Francesca Pelizzoli.
Rejoice at Easter: Illustrations from *This Amazing World* copyright © 2002 Ruth Rivers.
Peter the Fisherman: First published in *Stories of the Saints*. Text copyright © 2001 Joyce Denham. Illustrations copyright © 2001 Judy Stevens.
Easter is About: Text by Lois Rock first published in *The Lion Book of 1000 Prayers for Children*. Copyright © 2003 Lion Hudson. Illustrations from *The Story of the Cross* copyright © 2002 Gail Newey.
I Wish Tonight: First published by Lion as a picture story book with this title in 1999. Text copyright © 1999 Lion Hudson. Illustrations copyright © 1999 Anne Wilson.